Regency Romance:
The Fashion of the Season

An Unofficial Coloring Book for fans of the world of Bridgerton

Illustrated by: Jennifer Nicole Perz

Published 2023

Color Swatch Page

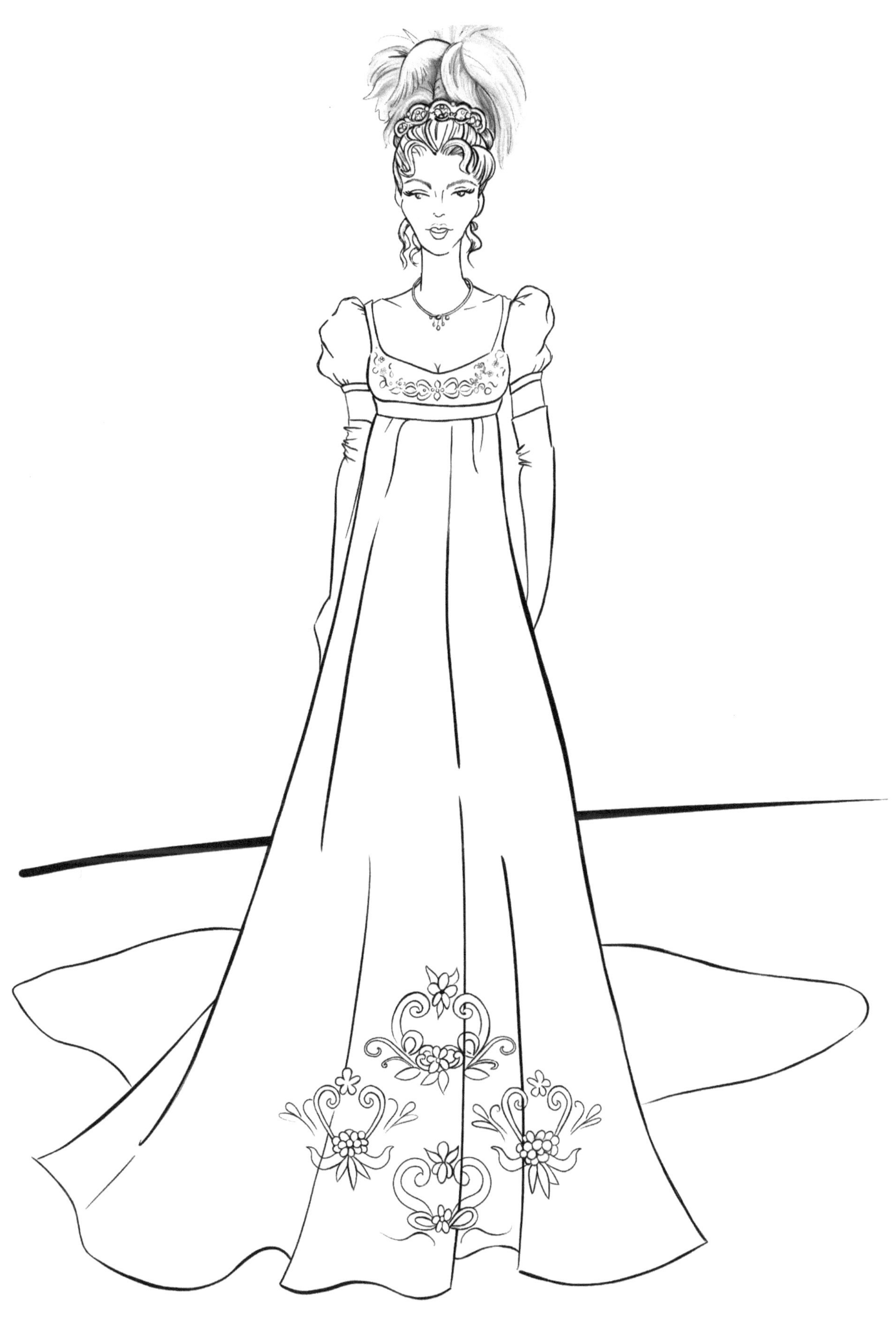

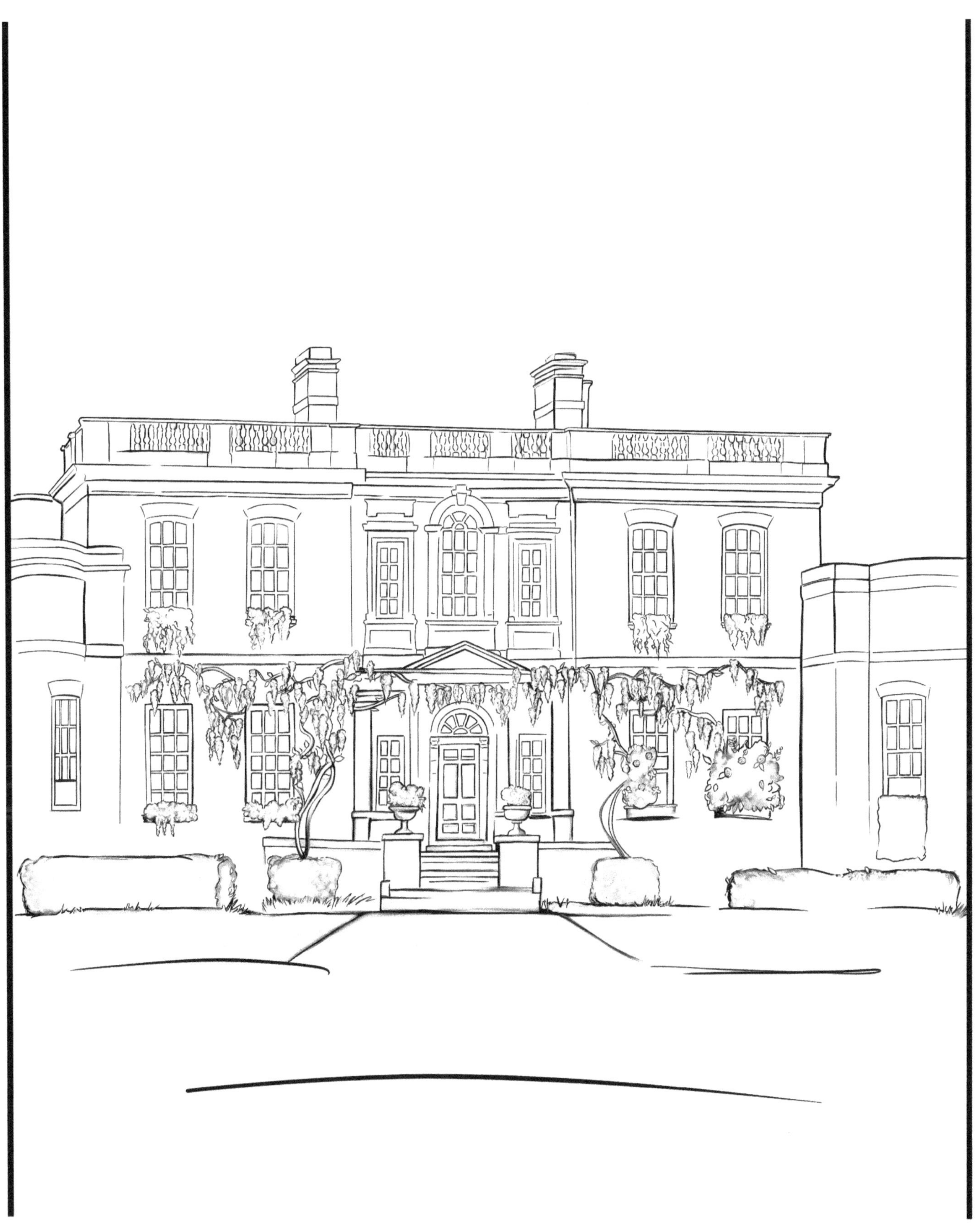

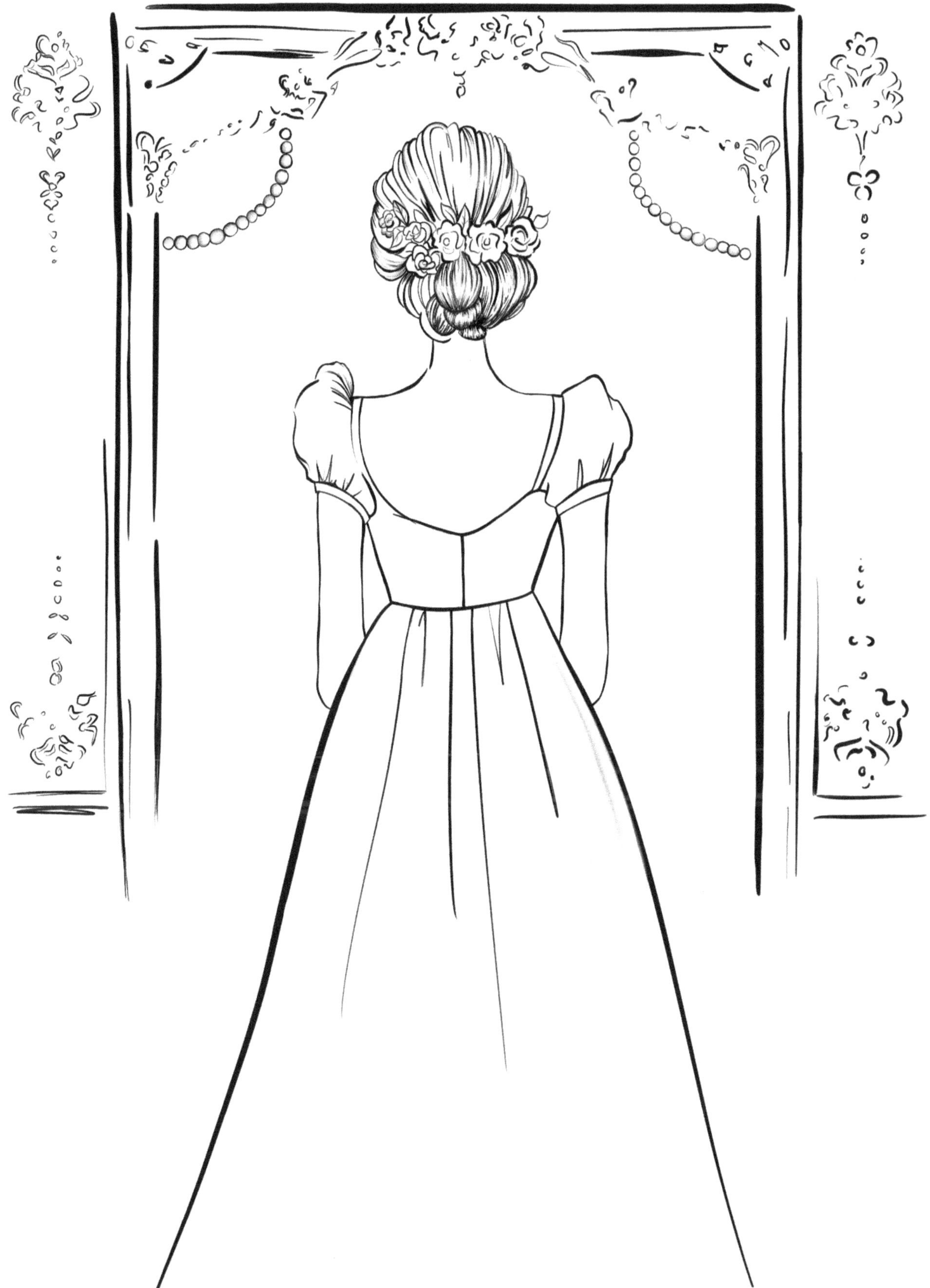

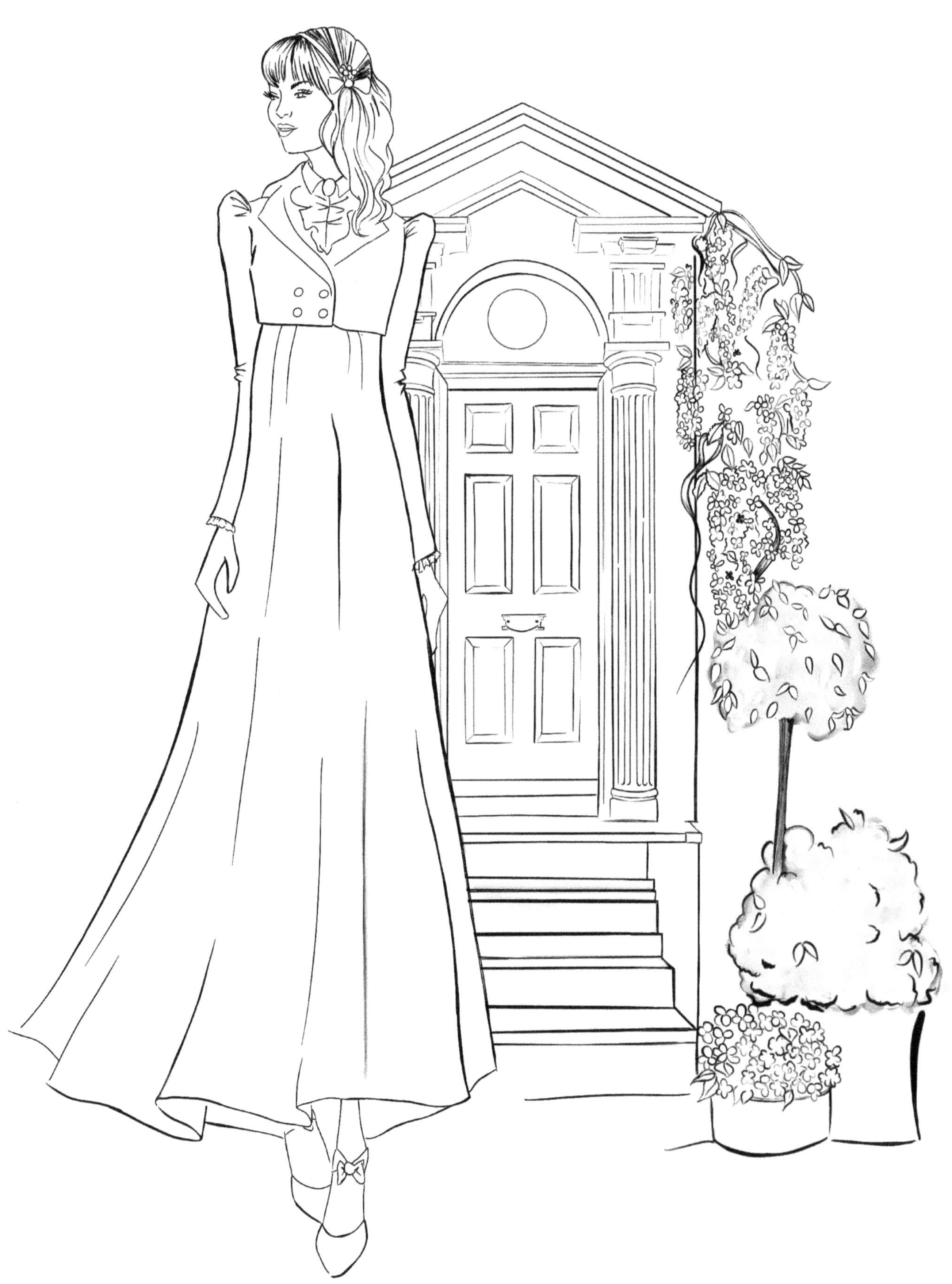

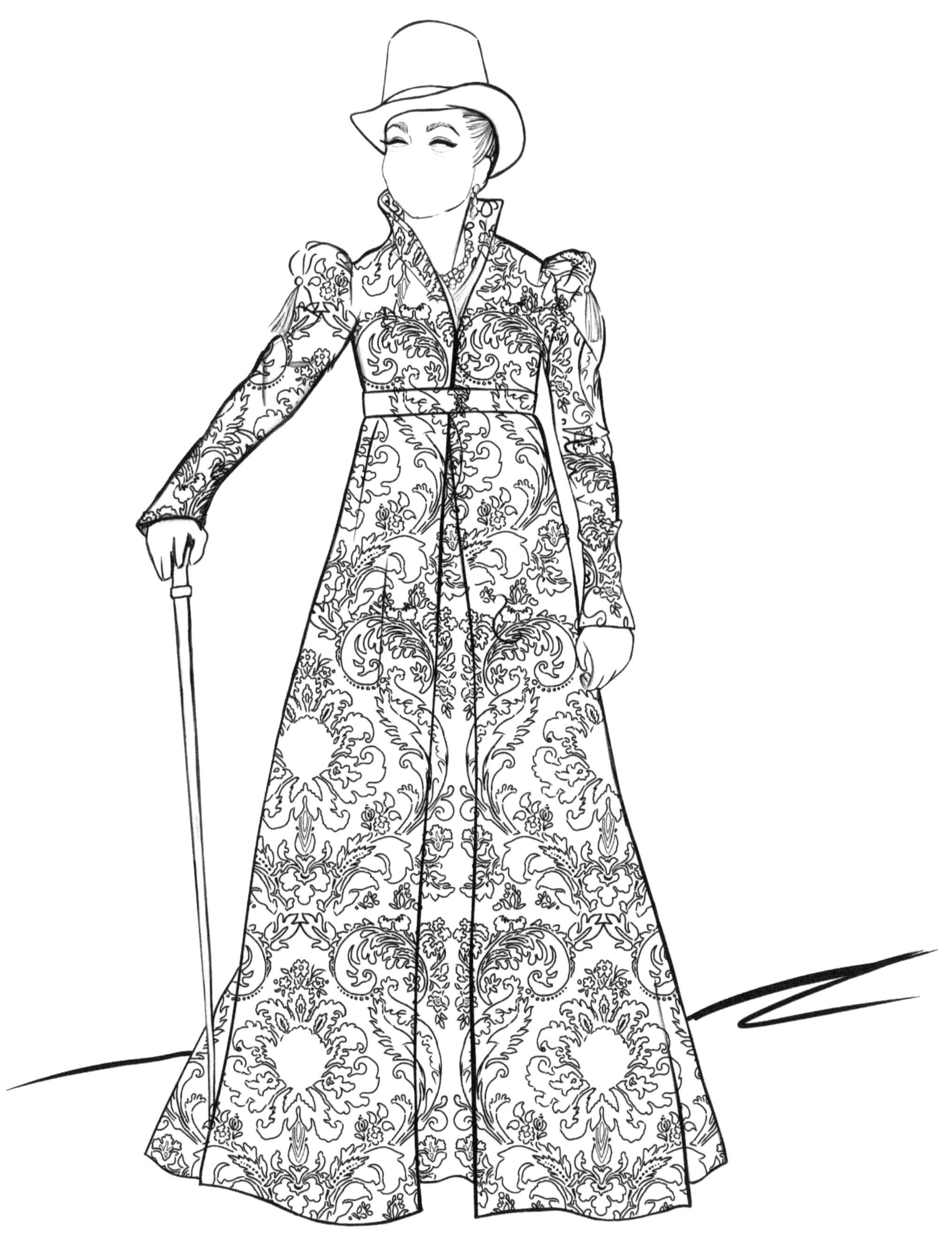

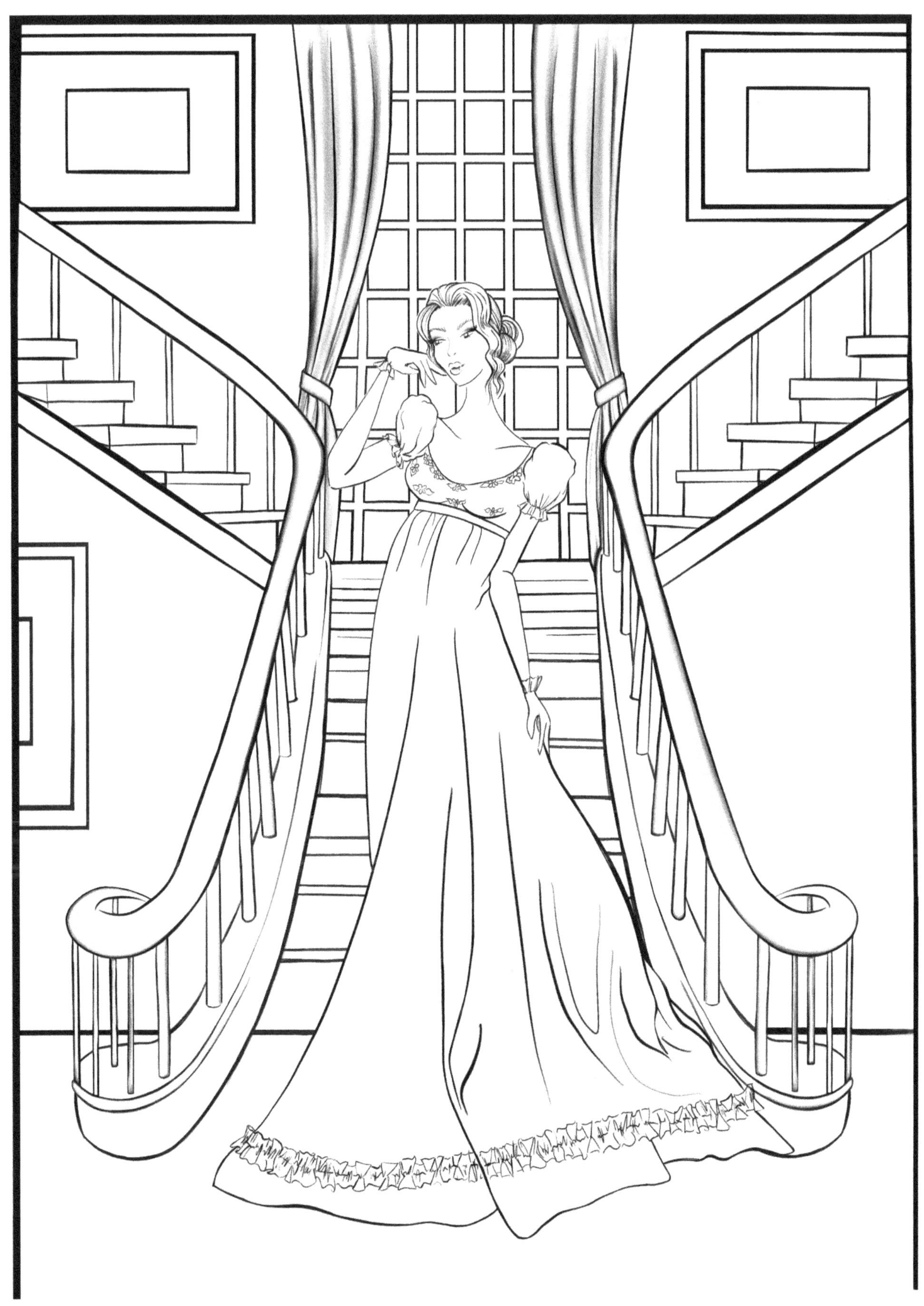

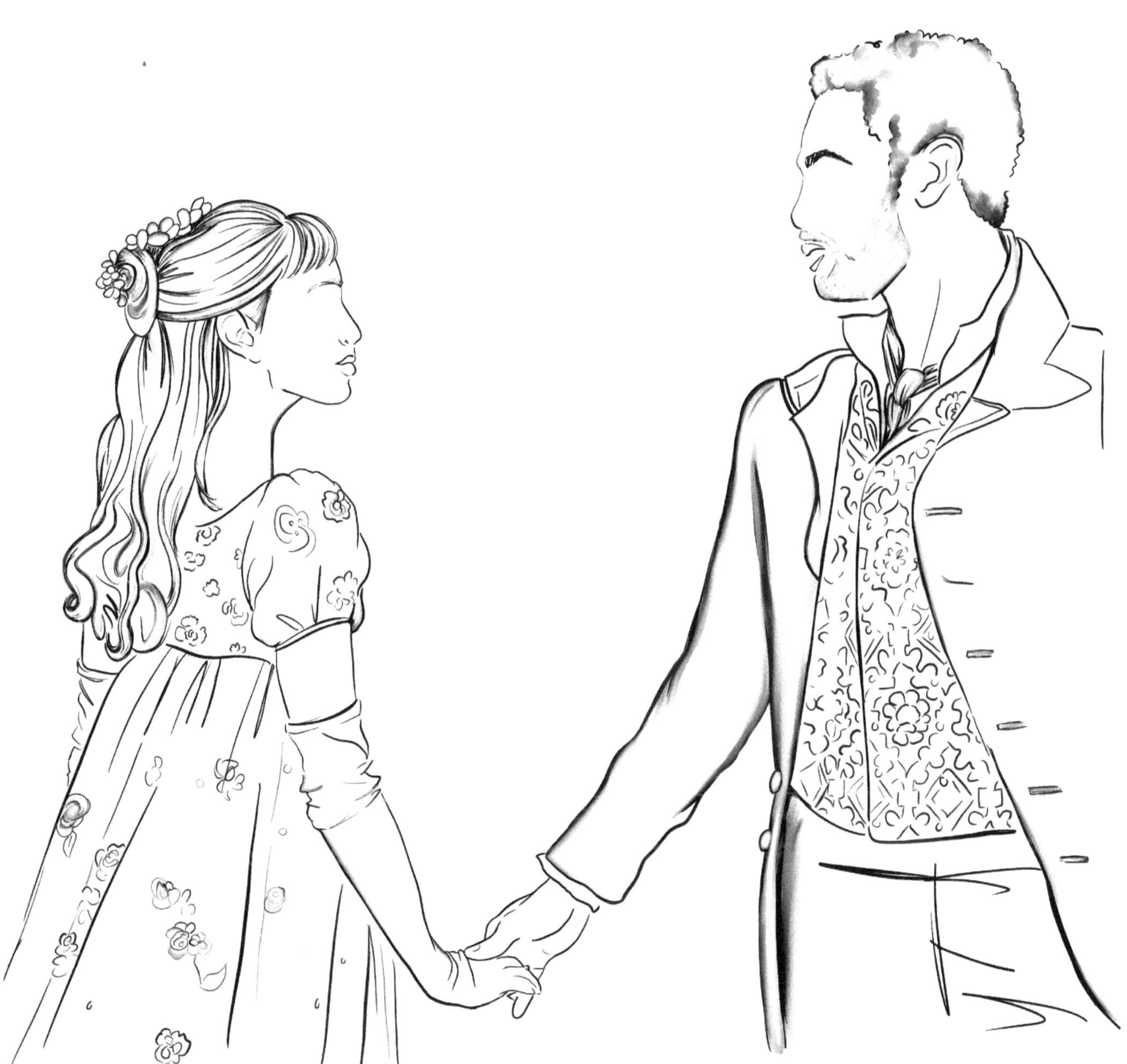

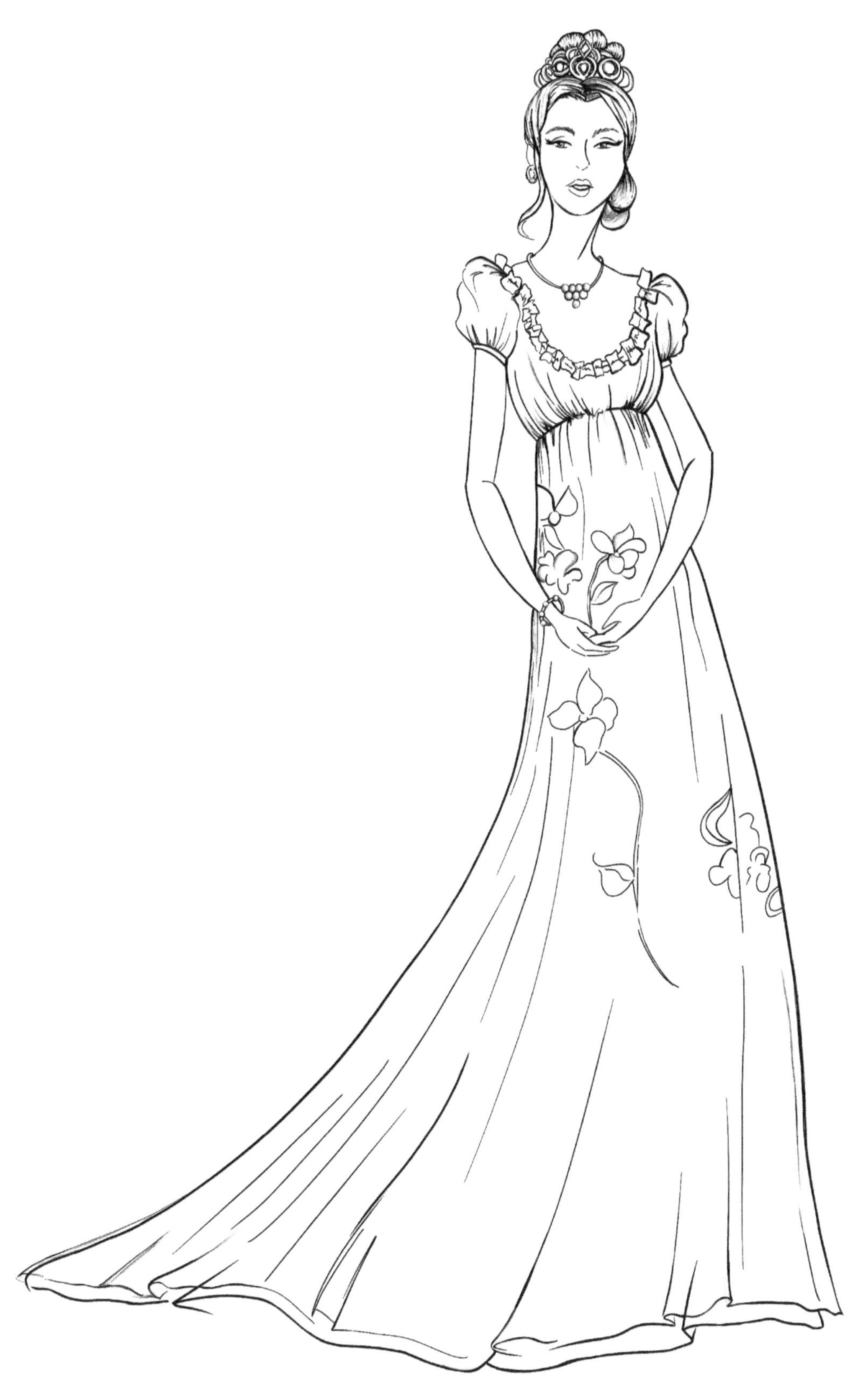

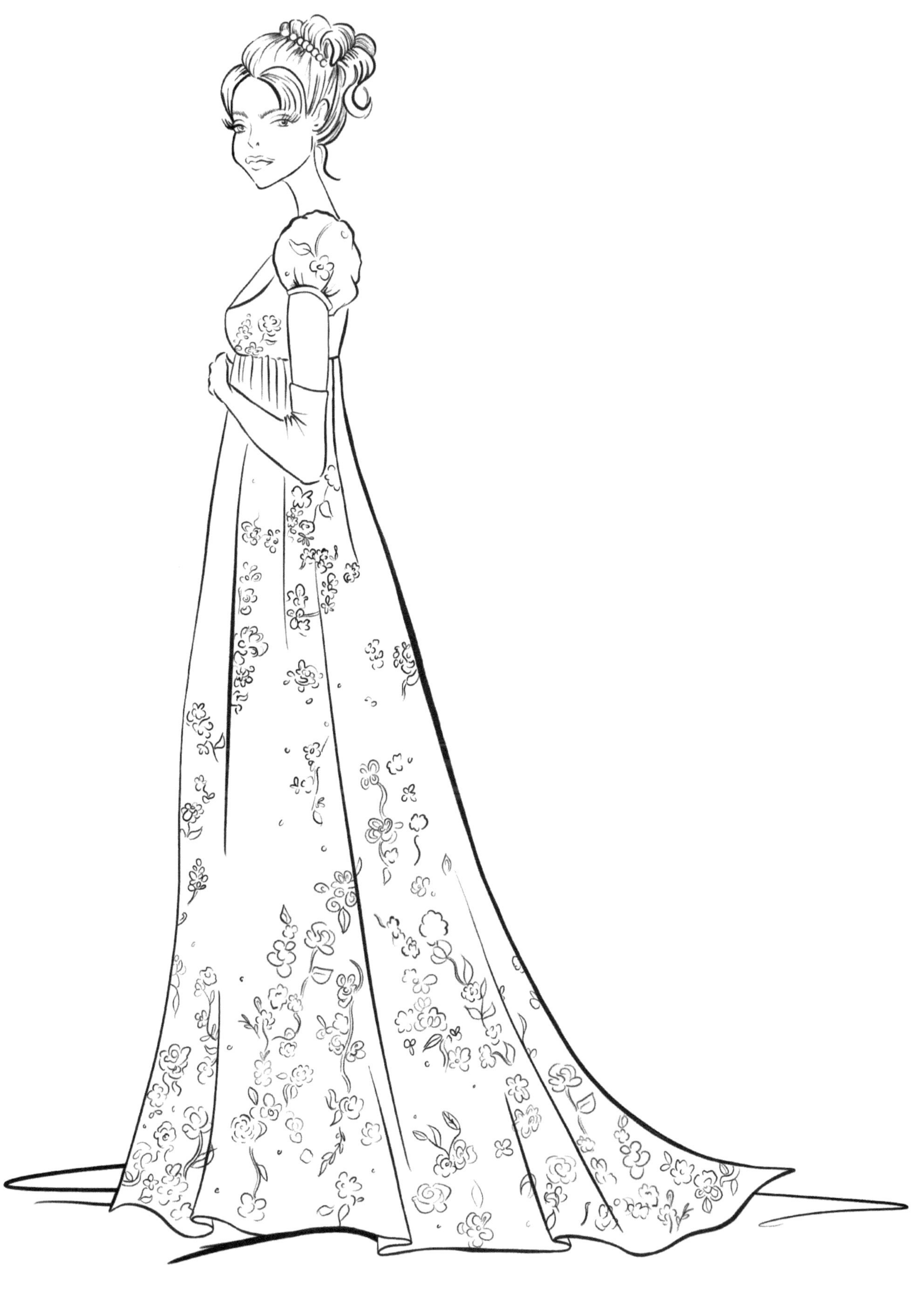

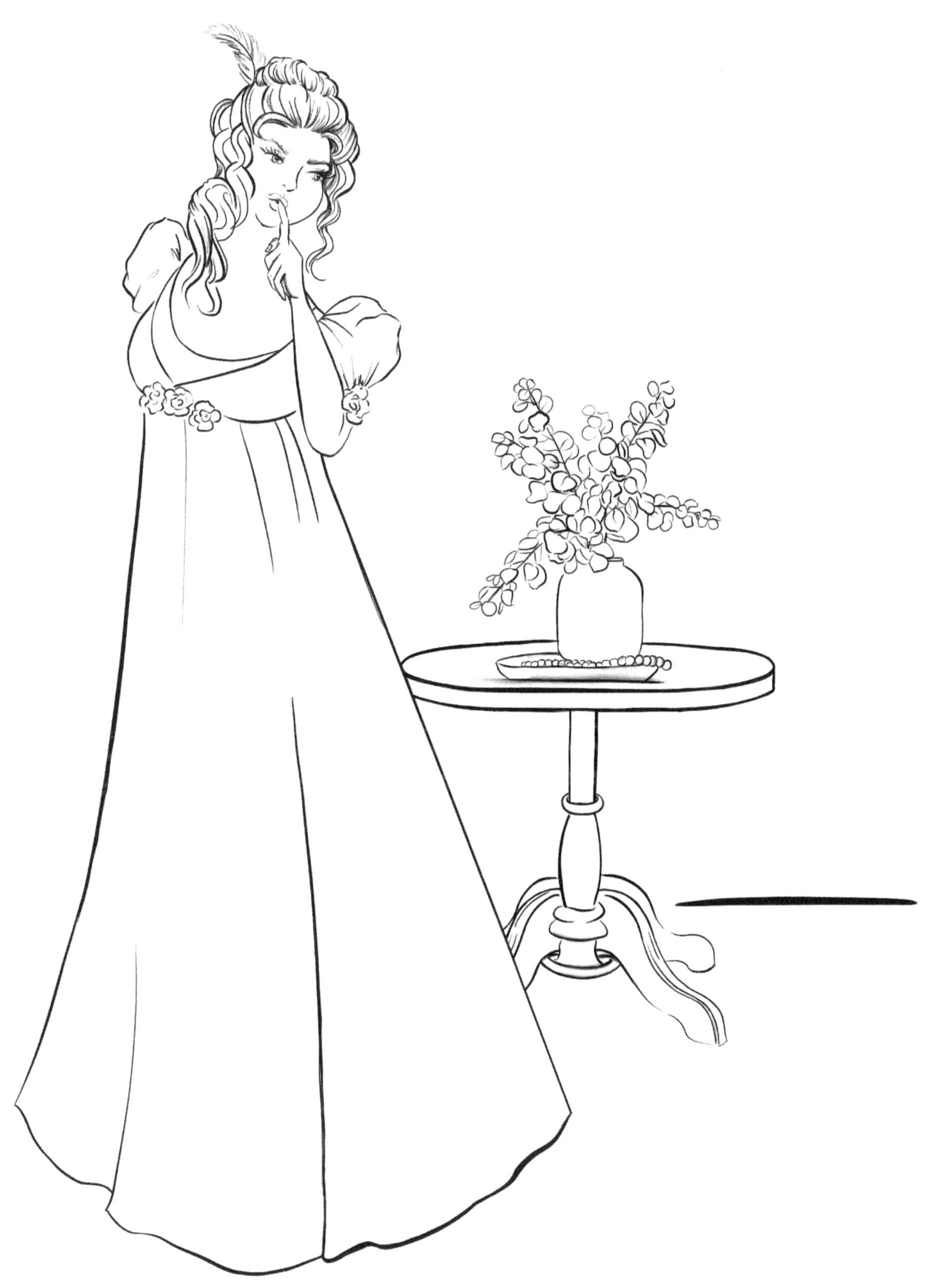

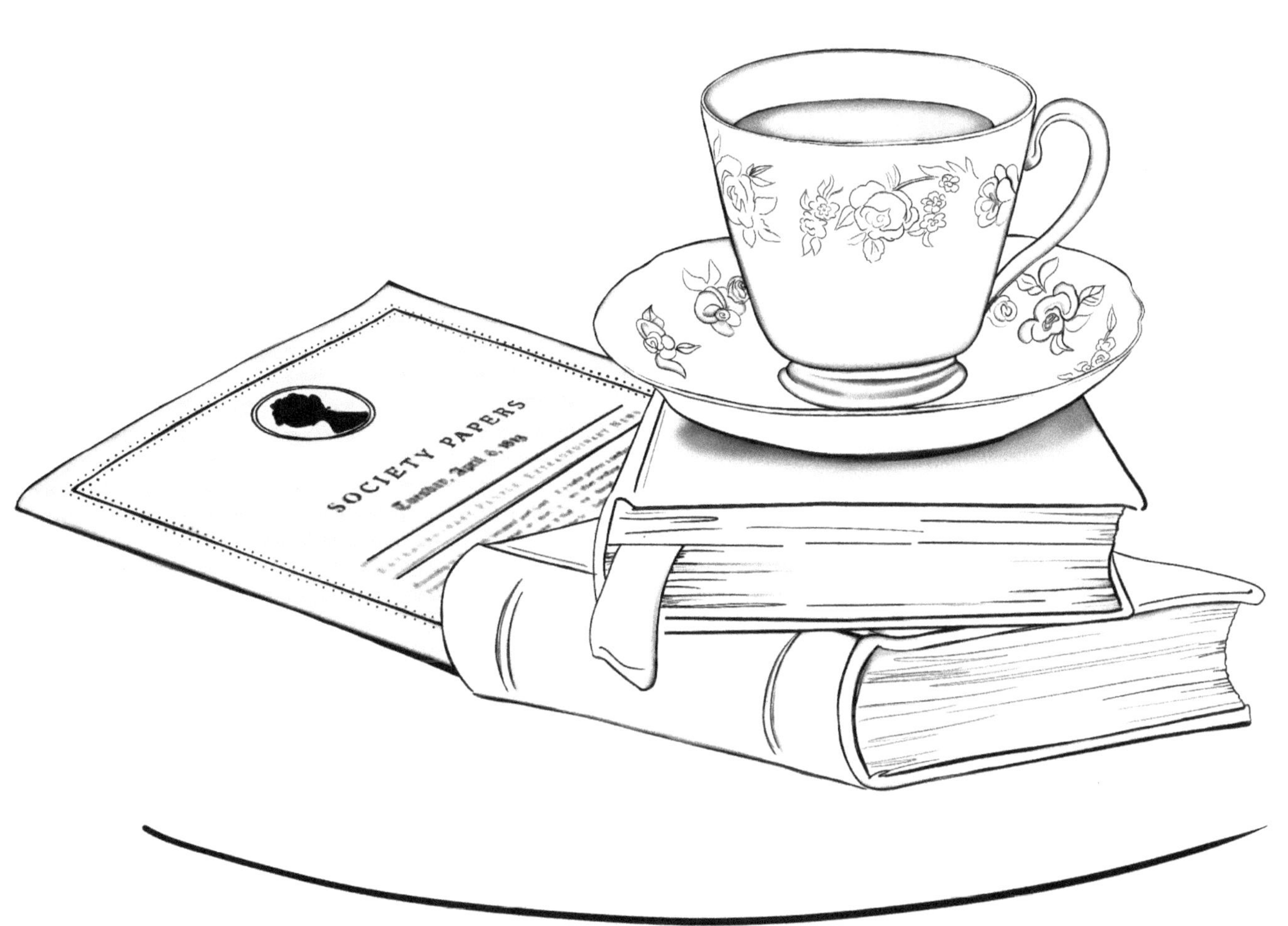

SOCIETY PAPERS
London, April 6, 1813

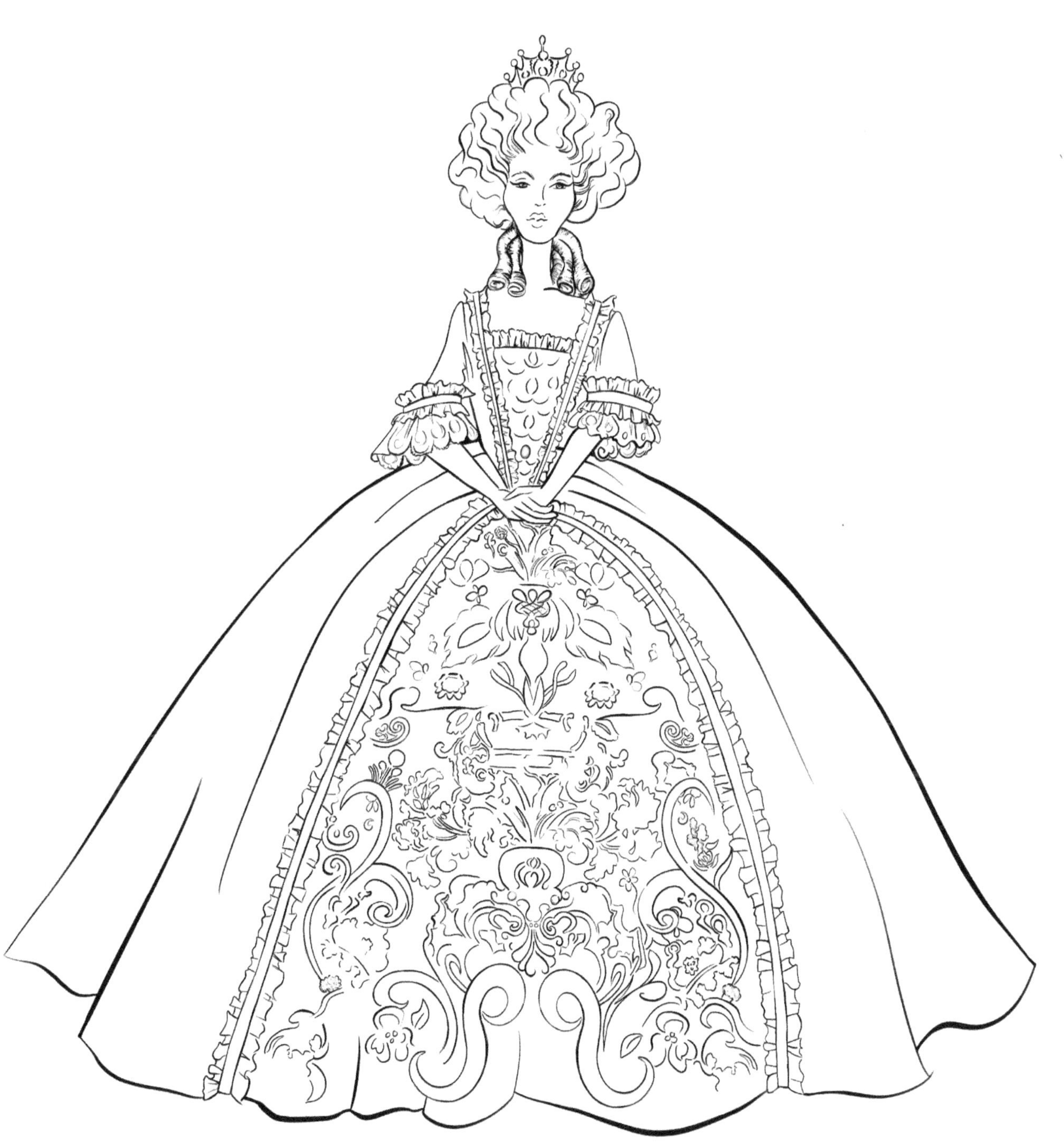

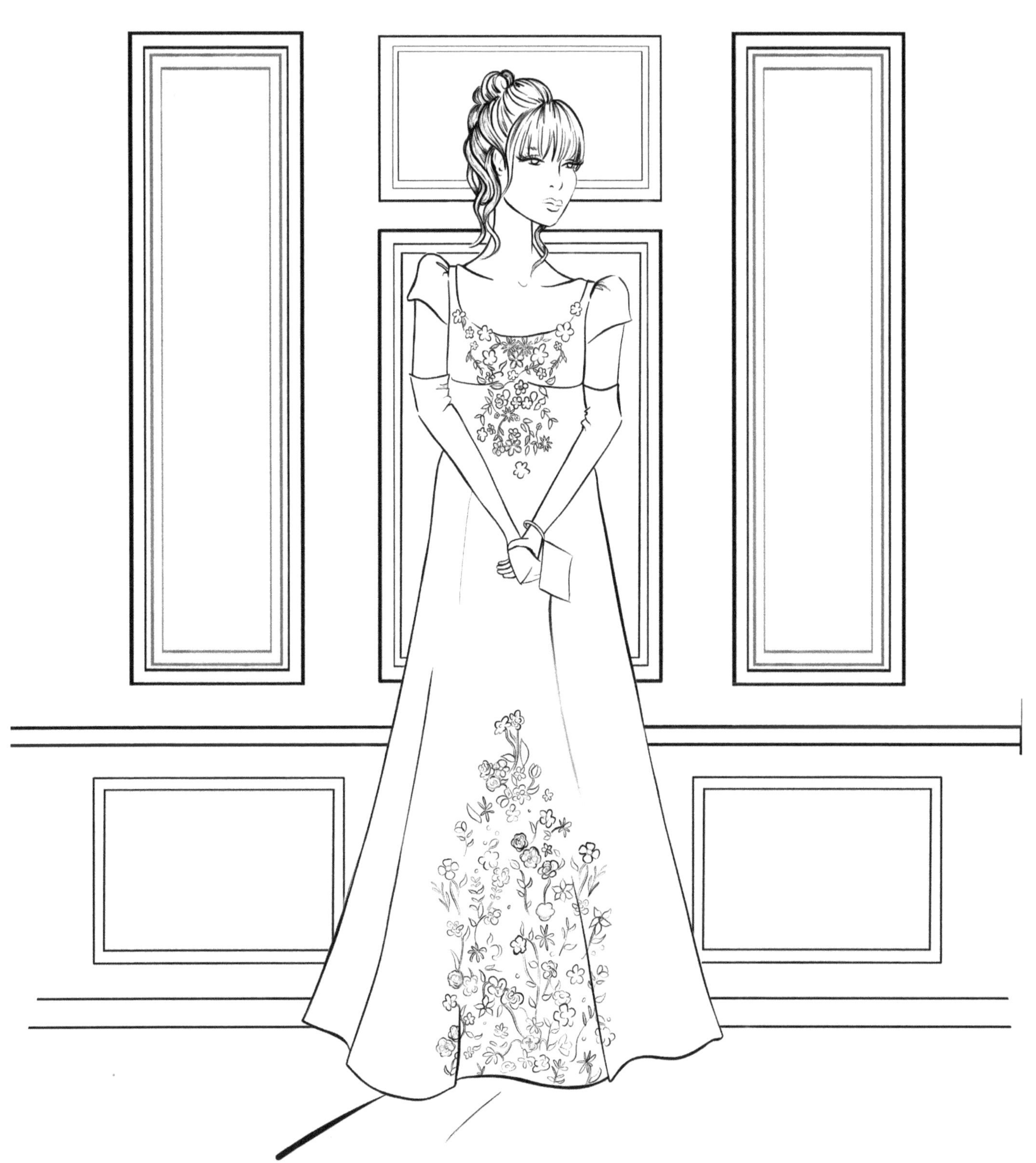

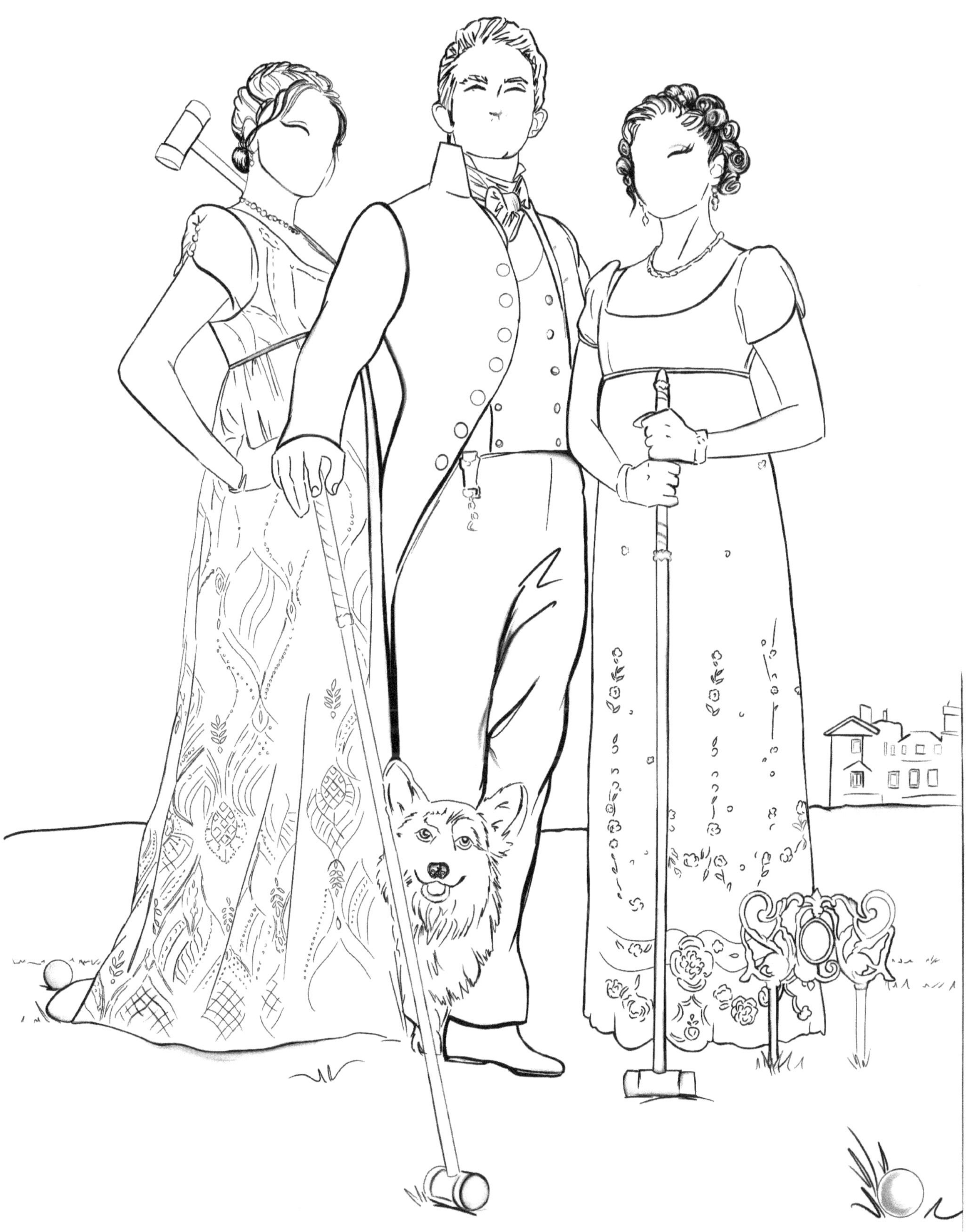

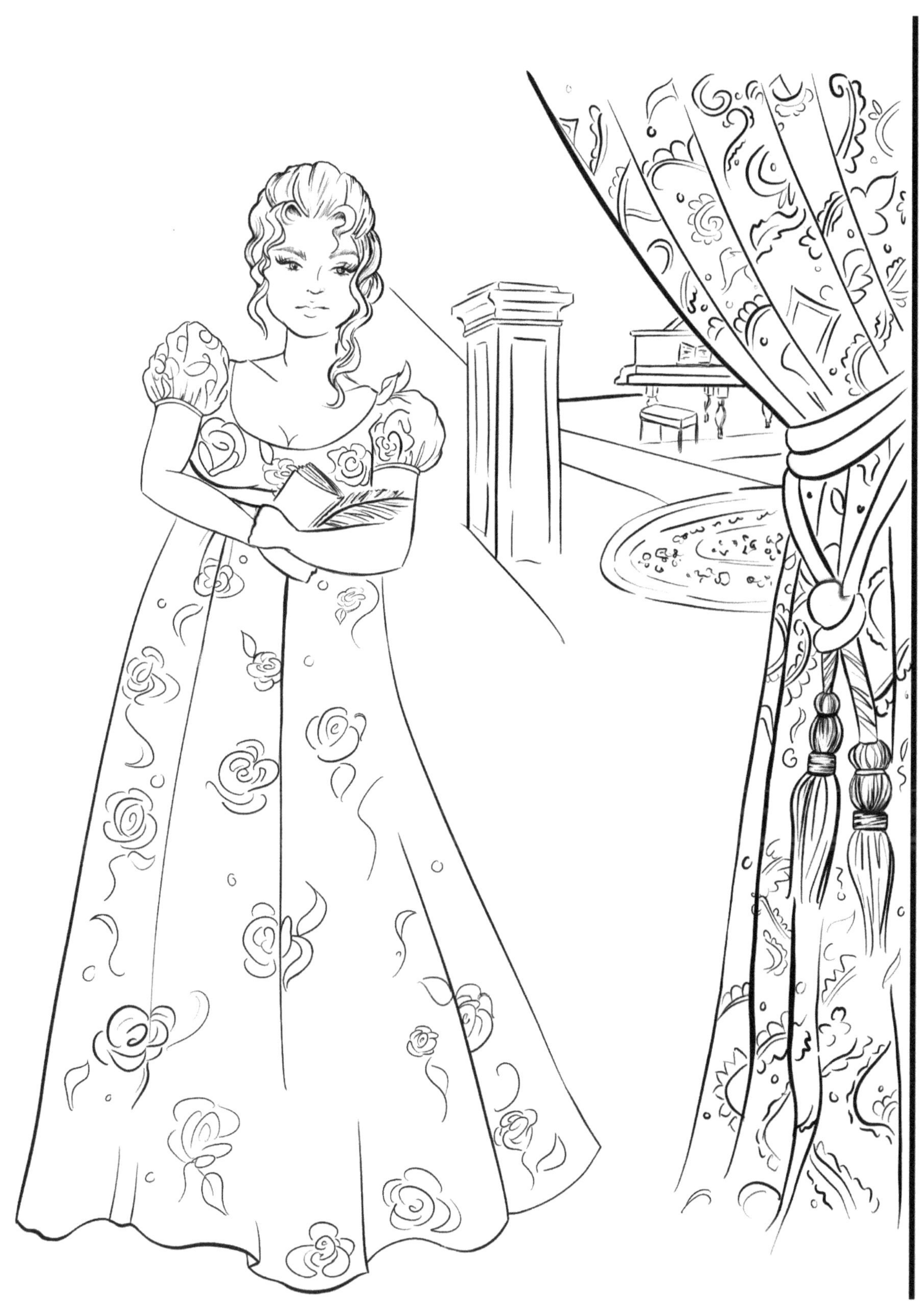

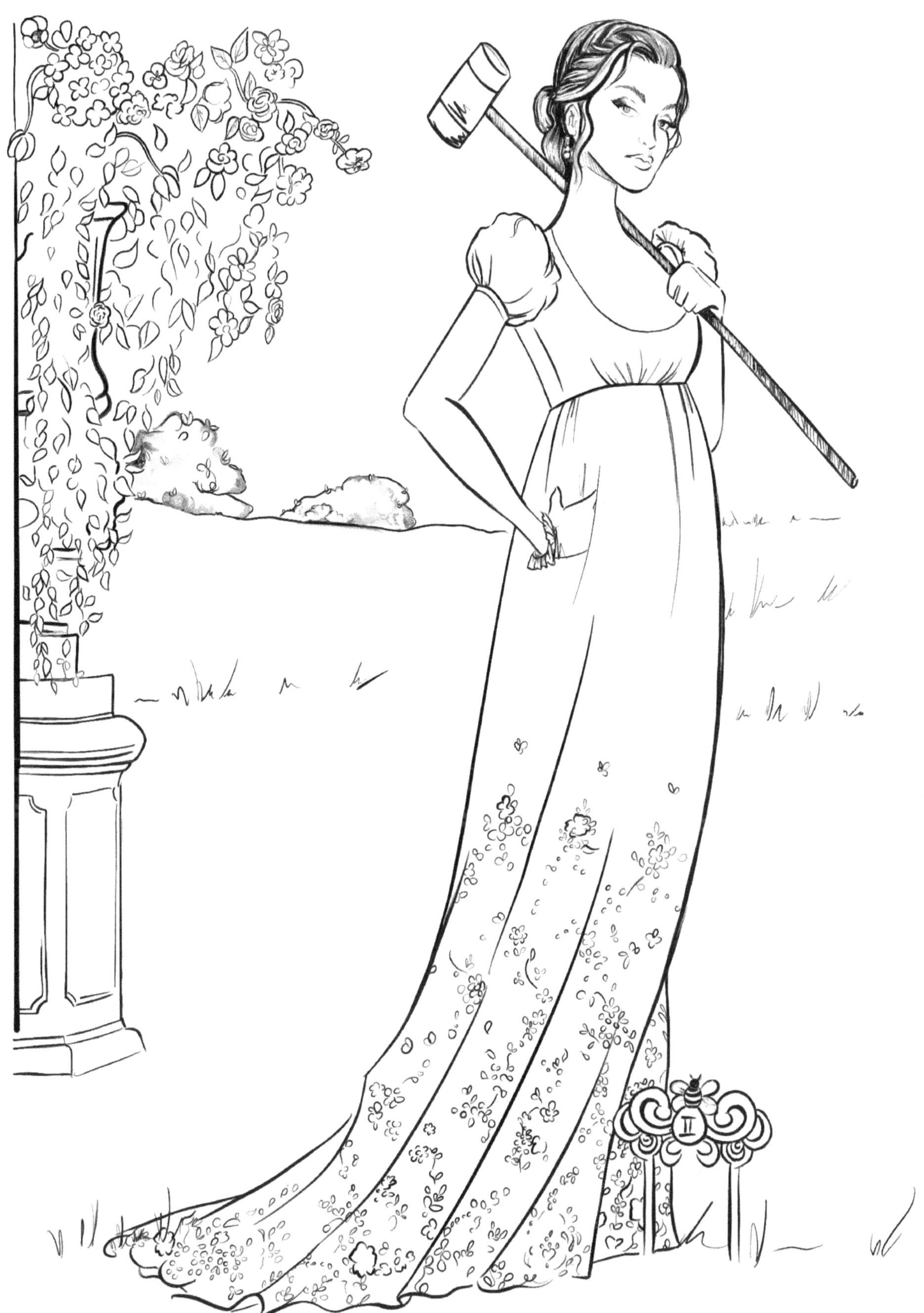

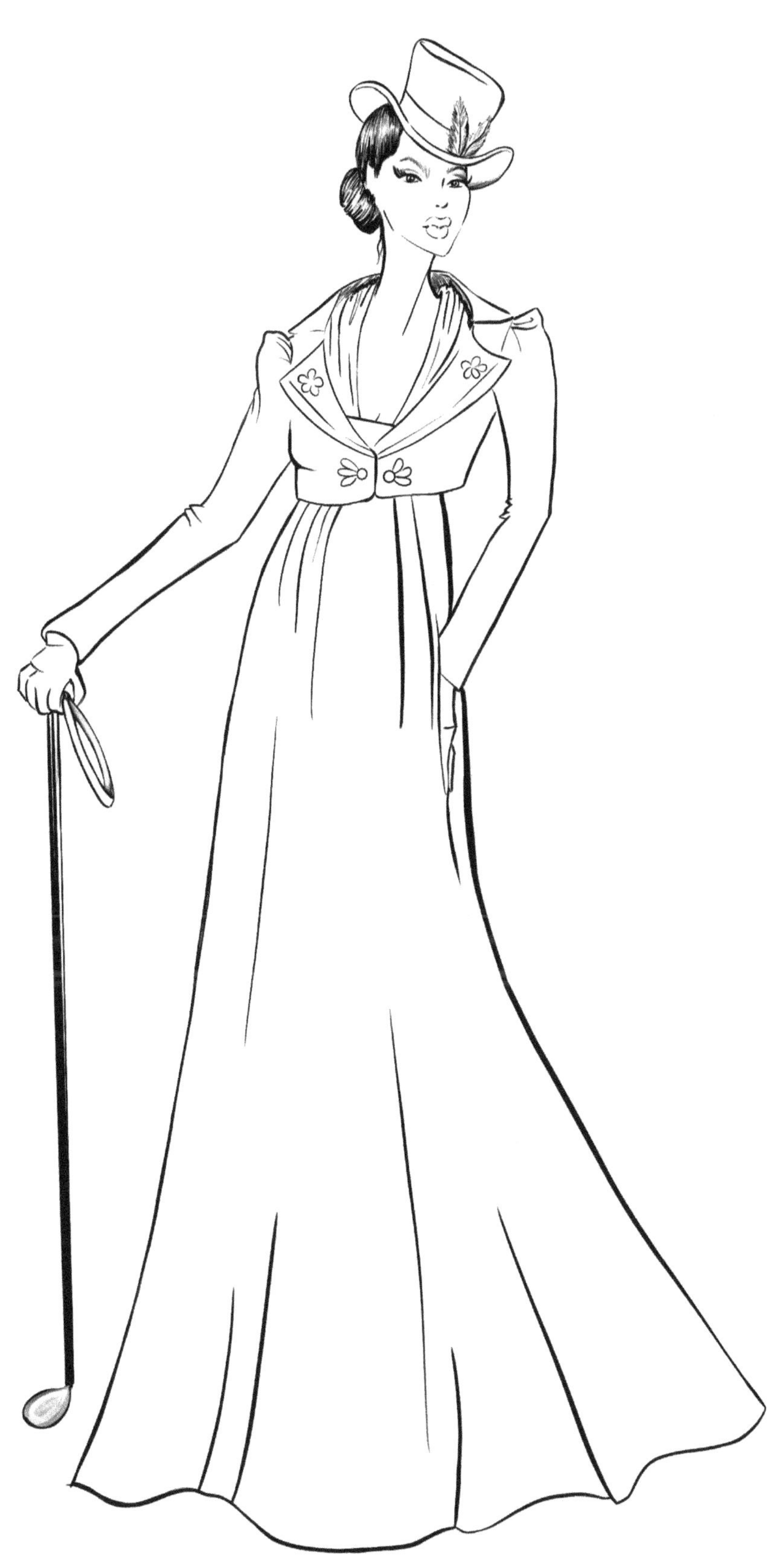

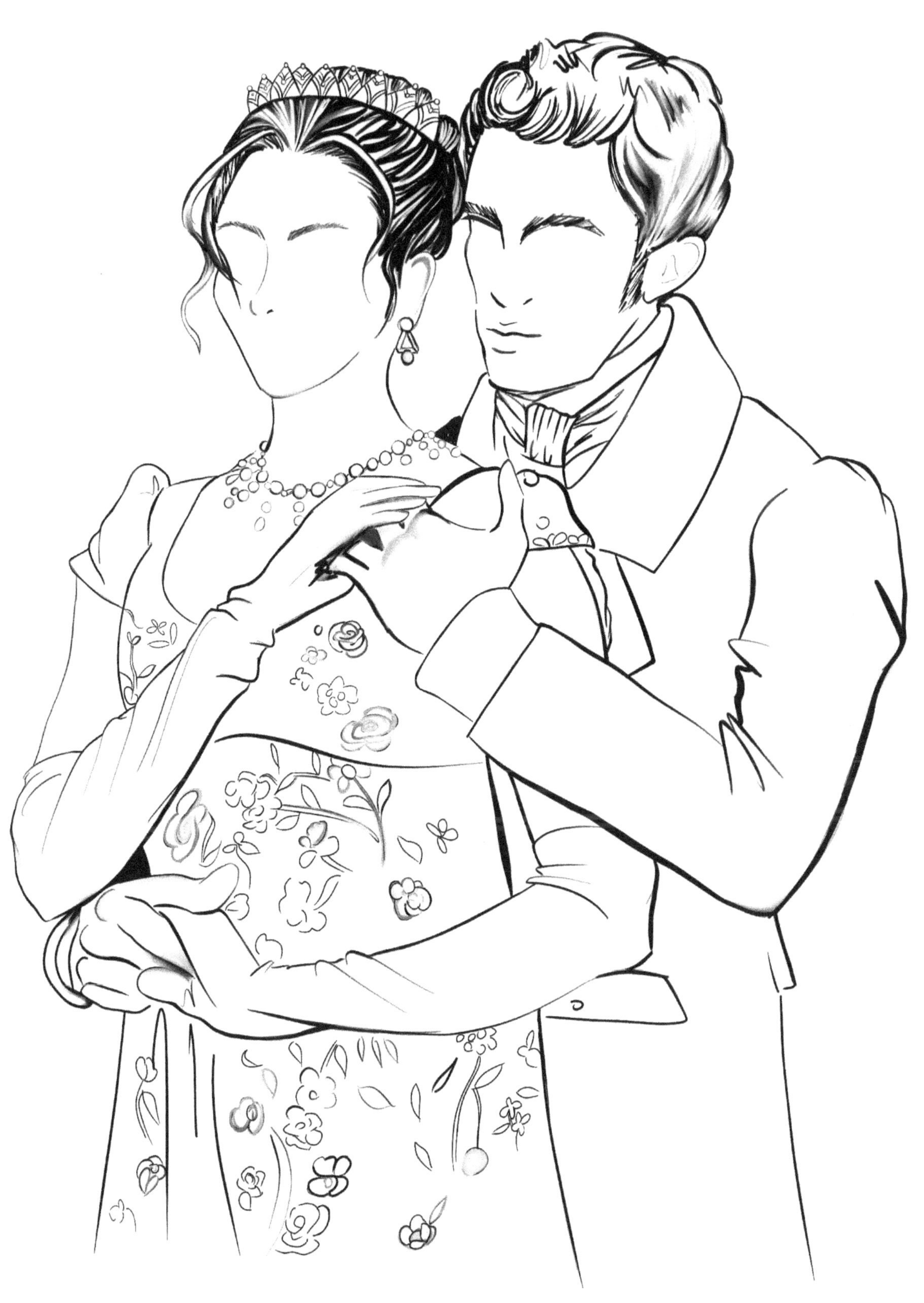

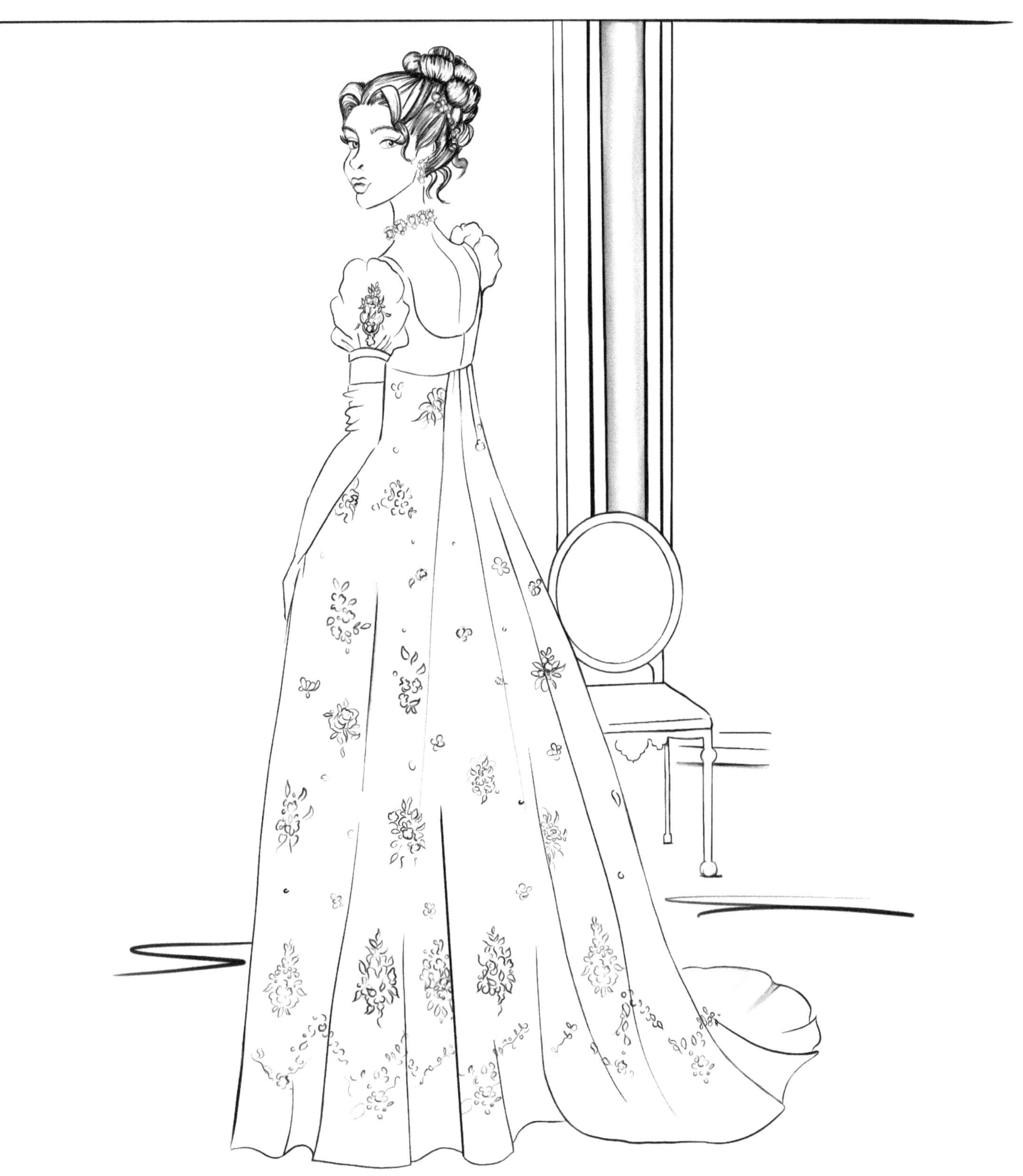

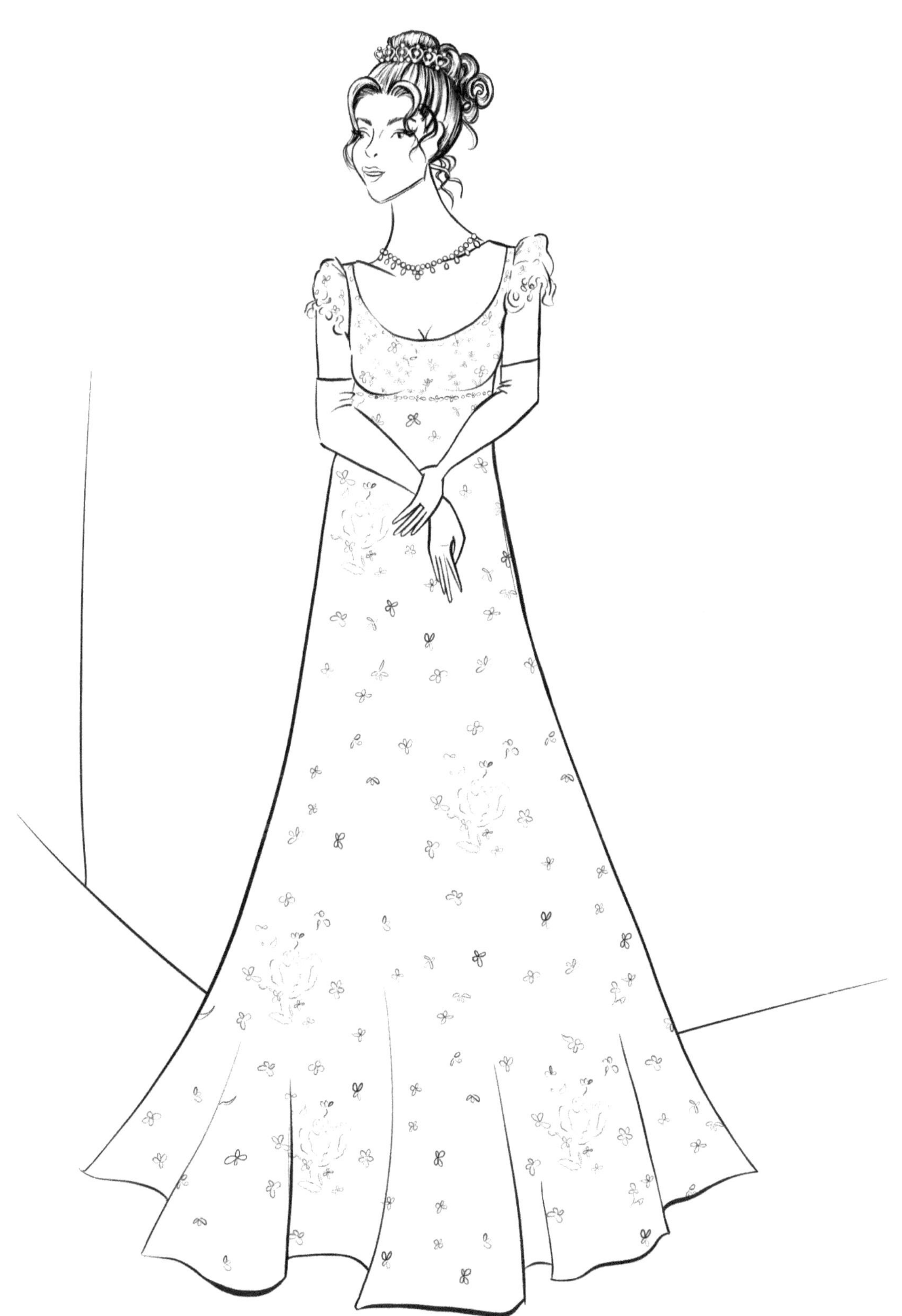

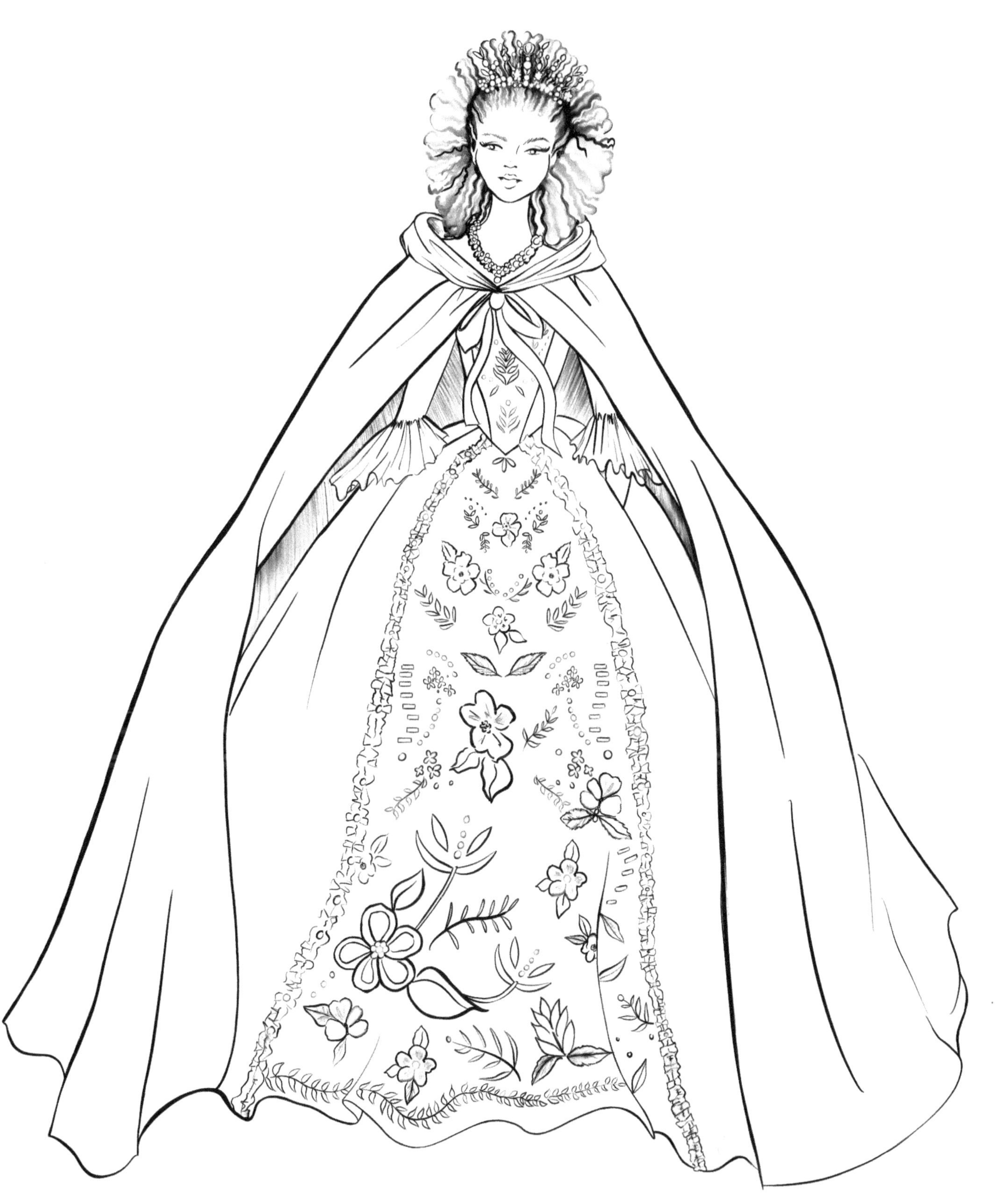

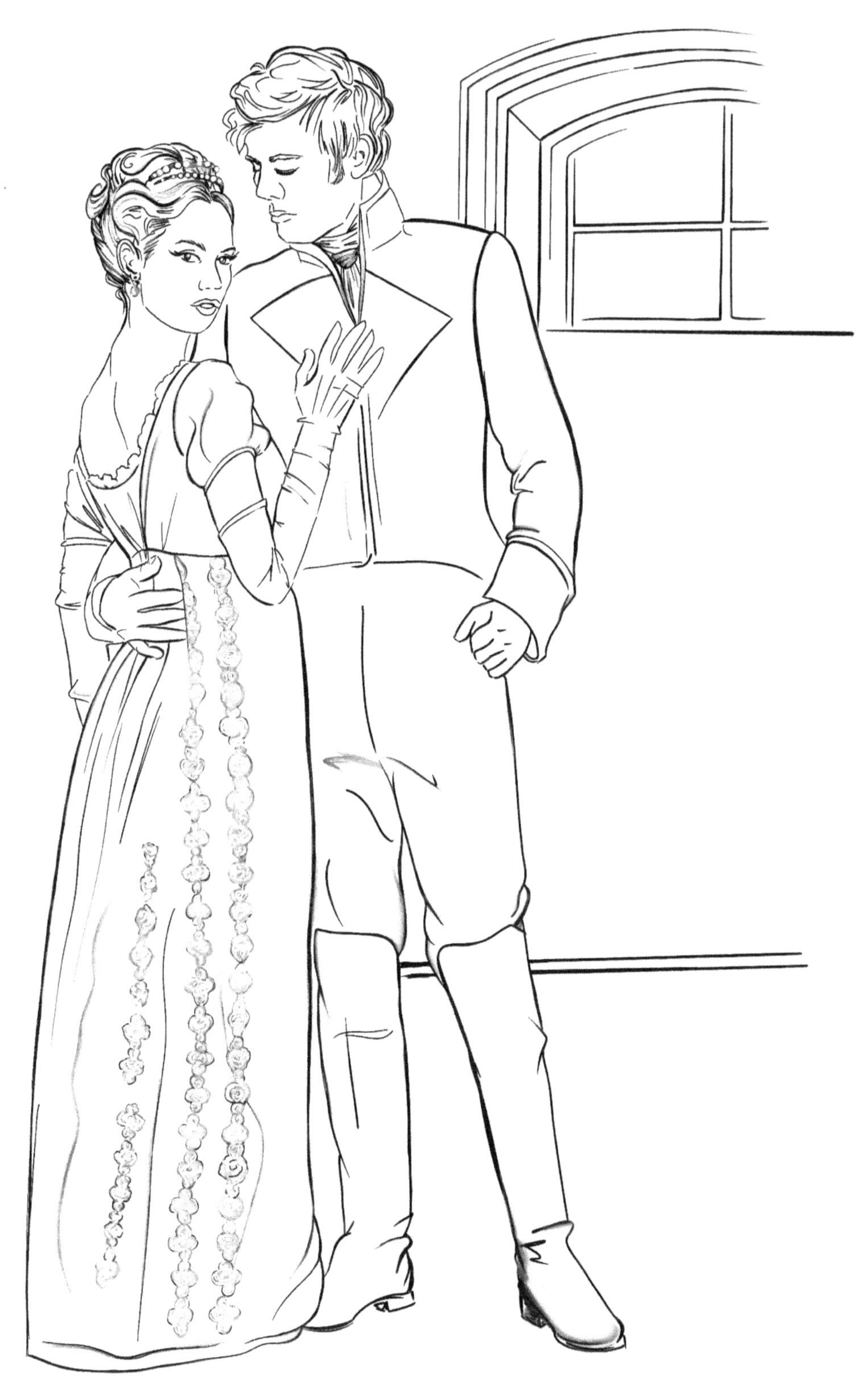

Sketches